A souvenir guide

Disraeli and Hughenden

Buckinghamshire

D0319387

National Trust

The home of the most unlikely Victorian Prime Minister

Benjamin Disraeli has always divided opinion but even his detractors do not deny his fascination. He was at once an ambitious orator and a flamboyant flatterer, in all assured of his own brilliance. Disraeli dazzled Victorian Britain through his politics, his novels, his close relationships and his reputation.

Tradition and change

Disraeli's Jewish heritage and his lack of public schooling or aristocratic background always set him apart. Being regarded as an outsider and an upstart may have deepened Disraeli's determination to succeed, but he suffered both physically and mentally from the slurs against him.

He had a deep respect for the aristocracy, perhaps partly because he was not born into it. He believed firmly in the benefits of the connection between political authority and the ownership of land. The aristocracy, like the church and the monarchy, was a structure that could create an ordered, responsible, and therefore strong, society. Disraeli was at heart a romantic and a traditionalist, but he also believed that 'change is inevitable in a progressive country. Change is constant.'

Political ambition

At the start of Disraeli's political career he met Lord Melbourne at a party. After some discussion Lord Melbourne asked his colourful young companion: 'Well now, what do you want to be?' Much to Lord Melbourne's surprise, Disraeli replied, 'I want to be Prime Minister'.

Disraeli was driven primarily by his ambition. As his career developed, he became known for his slippery and often self-serving political manoeuvres. He was tagged the 'sphinx without a riddle' and would have been most at home with the 'spin doctors' of contemporary politics. His most consistent belief was in his ability to become a great man, but he had to wait many years before the world caught up with his own conviction.

'A female friend'

Disraeli stated that he owed all the successes in his life to the women he knew. In financial terms, this was undoubtedly true, as his alliances with older women supported his political campaigns and novels, and helped to pay his considerable debts. It was a gift from Mrs Brydges Willyams that enabled him to pay for Hughenden. His charm was always apparent. The 21-year-old daughter of the Earl of Lindsay wrote in her diary on meeting Disraeli in 1834: 'The brilliance of my companion affected me and we ran on about poetry and Venice and Baghdad and Damascus and my eye lit up and my cheek burned.'

Disraeli's ability to listen, flatter and empathise helped him to forge intense and intimate bonds with women. He was a conscientious correspondent and enjoyed the confidences of his female friends, who included Queen Victoria.

At home at Hughenden

Disraeli's marriage to Mary Anne Wyndham Lewis and the home they created together at Hughenden gave him the fundamental grounding he needed to succeed. Acquiring a country house estate secured the status of Disraeli as a serious politician. Mary Anne devoted herself to running an efficient household and unreservedly supporting Disraeli's career, for which he was always grateful.

Hughenden became a retreat for Disraeli. For several months each year he divided his time here between his books and the trees on his estate; nature continued to inspire and comfort Disraeli for the remainder of his life.

Left Poster for one of Disraeli's election campaigns

Opposite The South Lawn

Below The young Disraeli; by Daniel Maclise

Timeline

1804	21 December: born in London
1826	*Vivian Grey* published
1830–1	Tour of the Mediterranean
1832	Defeated as the Radical Independent Candidate for High Wycombe
1837	Becomes Conservative MP for Maidstone
1839	Marries Mary Anne Wyndham Lewis
1841	MP for Shrewsbury
1844	*Coningsby* published
1845	*Sybil* published
1846	Splits Tory party by leading a group of aristocratic rebels against his own Prime Minister, Sir Robert Peel, over the repeal of the Corn Laws
1847	MP for Buckingham
1848	Buys Hughenden
1849	Conservative leader in House of Commons
1852	Chancellor of the Exchequer
1867	2nd Reform Bill, which brings the vote to the working man
1868	Briefly Prime Minister. Mary Anne made Viscountess Beaconsfield in her own right
1870	*Lothair* published
1872	Death of Mary Anne Disraeli
1874	At 70 'climbs to the top of the greasy pole' and becomes Prime Minister with working majority
1874–80	At home: introduces progressive policies like the Public Health Act. Abroad: an aggressive imperialist, acquiring a share in the Suez Canal
1876	Created Earl of Beaconsfield
1878	Congress of Berlin: Disraeli's triumph, which sought to end conflict in the Balkans
1880	*Endymion* published
1880	Defeated by Gladstone
1881	19 April: dies in London; buried at Hughenden

From a Pen and Ink Sketch by R. Moore James.]

THE

The foremost man of his age ; eminent in letters, in de

Right Print depicting the political life of Benjamin Disraeli

One man in his time plays many parts !

THE POLITICAL CAREER OF

IT HONOURABLE BENJAMIN DISRAELI, EARL OF BEACONSFIELD. K.G.

(Familiarly dubbed " Dizzy," as caricatured by " Scaramouch.")

a Statesman far-seeing and sagacious ; a patriot zealous for his country's honour ; a tried friend of Queen Victoria, by whom he was trusted, honoured, and mourned.

The outsider

When he became a politician, even within his own party, he was viewed with mistrust: 'There can be no doubt that there is a very strong feeling among Conservatives in the House of Commons against him. They are puzzled and alarmed by his mysterious manner, which has much of the foreigner about it.'

From Charles Greville's diary, 7 January 1848

Despite his conversion to Christianity, Disraeli was fiercely proud of his Jewish background, though it was often used against him. Further set apart by his early love of flamboyance and disregard for rules, he was viewed as an outsider by the Victorian establishment.

A mixed heritage

Disraeli possessed a romantic vision of his family's past, claiming they were from the most aristocratic branch of Sephardic Jews, who had escaped the Spanish inquisition and found refuge in Venice. His roots were actually much simpler: his grandfather came to England seeking employment in 1748, leaving behind two sisters looking after a Jewish school in the Venetian ghetto.

Disraeli was baptised with his siblings in 1817, when he was twelve. His father, Isaac D'Israeli, a kindly scholar with a vast personal library, converted his children to Christianity after falling out with his synagogue's authorities. This later enabled Disraeli to follow a parliamentary career, but political commentators and satirists of the day constantly reminded him of his roots and his difference.

He was a determined supporter of Jewish rights against prevailing prejudice, commenting: 'They are not a new people, who have just got into notice, and who, if you do not recognise their claims, will disappear.'

Schooling

Unlike other successful politicians of the day, Disraeli had attended neither public school nor university. He was educated principally at Higham Hall near Walthamstow, where his passion for romance and adventure stories, combined with an inventive imagination, set him apart from more studious pupils. It was only when he was fifteen and allowed to study at home that he became a conscientious student, devoted to the classics.

Left Portrait of Isaac D'Israeli by Daniel Maclise

Disraeli the dandy

As a young man, Disraeli's flamboyant manner and style of dress always provoked comment. His friend Bulwer-Lytton noted that he wore 'green velvet trousers, a canary coloured waistcoat, low sleeves, silver buckles, lace at his wrists, his hair in ringlets'.

His peacock-like display set him apart. Lord Byron was a strong influence. After meeting the poet through his father's publisher, John Murray, Disraeli was captivated by Byron's exuberant dress and excessive lifestyle. He had a weakness for what was seen as bad company.

In his twenties, Disraeli enjoyed a Grand Tour of the Eastern Mediterranean. He luxuriated in his exotic encounters; in a letter to his early patron, Benjamin Austen, he wrote: 'For a week I was in a scene equal to anything in the Arabian Nights ... I am quite a Turk, wear a Turban, smoke a pipe six feet long and squat on a divan.' He also wrote to his sister complaining that he didn't find travelling expensive, but 'I am ruined by my wardrobe'.

In his later years, Disraeli became the statesman; his use of hyperbole was controlled in line with his more sober attire. Yet his appearance still marked him out as different and as an outsider.

Above *Disraeli as the author of Vivian Grey*; engraving based on a drawing by Daniel Maclise

Left The motto on the Beaconsfield coat of arms translates: 'To the brave, nothing is too difficult'

The writer

Disraeli enjoyed a successful career as a writer of 'silver fork' novels, containing thinly disguised descriptions of individuals in high society. Disraeli's work provided satirical comment on society and was frequently autobiographical. He wrote twelve novels and other shorter fictional works as well as non-fiction and a political biography.

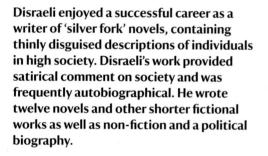

Early influences

Disraeli's father was a popular author of poems, novels, satires and short stories as well as volumes of literary criticism and created a great library at Bradenham. Isaac was bookish rather than a great intellect, but moved in literary circles, dining with the publisher John Murray and celebrated by Sir Walter Scott and Lord Byron. As a young man, Benjamin Disraeli shared, and was influenced by, his father's literary associations.

Early novels

Disraeli's first novel, the autobiographical *Vivian Grey*, was published anonymously in 1826–7 in two parts. When it was revealed that Disraeli was the author, he was slated for being a swindler and a Jew and not the fashionable man of society that the novel had indicated. 'I was sacrificed, I was scalped.... the criticism fell from my hand, a film floated over my vision; my knees trembled.'

The hero of *Vivian Grey* comments, 'There is no fascination so irresistible to a boy as the smile of a married woman.' A sentiment that remained true for Disraeli throughout his life.

Above Leather-bound books from Disraeli's collection

Left Manuscript of Disraeli's *Sybil*

The Right Honorable Benjamin Disraeli

The Right Honorable Benjamin Disraeli

'My books are the history of my life;
I don't mean a vulgar photograph
of incidents, but the psychological
development of my character.
Self-inspiration may be egotistical
but it is generally true.'

Disraeli to Lady Bradford

The criticism of Disraeli's work contributed to
his nervous collapse aged 22. It was several
years before he recovered fully, and he became
ashamed of the novel that betrayed the excesses
of his youth. However, his work continued to
reflect his life: *Henrietta Temple* (1837) was
inspired by his affair with Henrietta Sykes.

Political novels

In the 1840s Disraeli published a trilogy of
novels attacking the Tory policy of his leader
Sir Robert Peel, beginning with *Coningsby, or
the New Generation* in 1844. *Sybil, or the Two
Nations* followed in 1845, and *Tancred, or the
New Crusade* in 1847. Throughout the three
books he argued for reform that turned away
from utilitarianism, towards a paternalistic
system that could instil social responsibility
to address the divide between rich and poor.
The novels argue that one nation can be
achieved through returning to traditional
structures and systems of the past.

Disraeli presented Queen Victoria with
a set of his novels in 1868 and acknowledged
her own literary achievements: 'We authors,
Ma'am….'

'When I want to read a novel,
I write one'

Disraeli

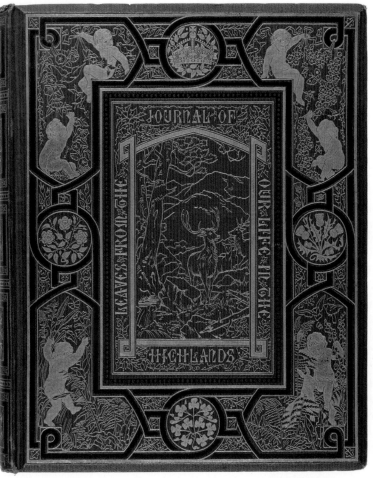

Later novels

Lothair (1870) is a romance and more subtle
and satirical than the impassioned political
works produced 20 years earlier. Similarly,
Endymion (1880) was a mature and mellow
novel depicting the transformative influence
of women on a man's political career. Both
works reflect the experience of an older man.

Disraeli's final but incomplete novel told the
story of a character named Falconet, and was
based on the life of his political enemy William
Gladstone. Only nine chapters were
completed, but they were sufficiently vitriolic
to show that Disraeli's attitude to Gladstone
had not mellowed with age.

Above *Leaves from the
Journal of our Life in the
Highlands from 1848–1861*,
written by Queen Victoria

Left Disraeli's bookplates

The ladies' man

Above Sarah D'Israeli; by Daniel Maclise

Disraeli's great ability to win over and charm extended beyond politics to his personal relationships. Throughout his life his closest friendships were with women. In particular, he formed profitable connections with older, wealthy married women. Disraeli often sought their maternal care and support, appreciating their affection as well as their money.

Henrietta Sykes

His first serious affair, in 1833, was with Henrietta Sykes, wife of Sir Francis Sykes, 3rd Baronet, of Basildon Park in Berkshire (now also in the care of the National Trust). Around 80 letters from Henrietta survive describing her passionate and somewhat maternal affection for Disraeli during their three-year relationship. When Henrietta was confronted by her husband, she countered his accusations with criticism of his own infidelity. As a consequence, her relationship with Disraeli continued, reluctantly sanctioned by her husband. The affair ended when Disraeli recognised the damage it was causing his career.

'Man is a predatory animal. The worthiest objects of his chase are women and power. After I married Mary Anne I desisted from the one and devoted my life to the other.'

Disraeli

Sarah D'Israeli

Perhaps the most consistently important woman in Disraeli's life was his sister, Sarah. Throughout his life, he sought her advice, and she shared his triumphs. William Meredith, Sarah's fiancé, died of smallpox whilst touring Egypt with Disraeli. After this, Sarah remained at the family home at Bradenham and never married, but lived through and for Disraeli. He continued to confide in his sister, writing: 'She was the harbour of refuge in all the storms of my life and I had hoped she would have closed my eyes.'

Mary Anne Disraeli

Disraeli first described Mary Anne as a 'pretty little woman, a flirt and a rattle'. She was the wealthy widow of Wyndham Lewis. She was talkative, energetic, volatile and eccentric but believed in Disraeli's capabilities from the start: 'Mark what I say... Mr Disraeli will in a very few years be one of the greatest men of his day.' They married in 1839. Mary Anne was 47, and Disraeli twelve years younger.

There is no doubt that Mary Anne's wealth attracted Disraeli; she brought the house at Grosvenor Gate to the marriage and paid off many of his debts. She also devoted her life to Disraeli, who was increasingly grateful for her loyalty and support. He was devastated by her death in 1872.

Sarah Brydges Willyams

Disraeli's friendship with an eccentric, older Jewish widow partly developed from their shared heritage. He sent her a copy of his novel *Tancred*, saying that it was a 'vindication of the race from which we alike spring'.

The Disraelis made annual visits to Mrs Brydges Willyams in Torquay, exchanged many letters and often sent presents of food or flowers. Disraeli agreed to become executor of her will and to her request that she be laid to rest at Hughenden church, where she is buried alongside Disraeli and Mary Anne. In return, Mrs Brydges Willyams left him £30,000 in her will, with which he was able to pay off the mortgage on Hughenden.

Lady Chesterfield and Lady Bradford

After Mary Anne died, Disraeli found comfort in the friendship of two sisters, Anne, Countess of Chesterfield and Selina, Countess of Bradford. Lady Chesterfield was a widow two years older than Disraeli, whilst Lady Bradford was seventeen years younger than her sister. The outpourings of affection, complaints of neglect and tender words of forgiveness that Disraeli ceaselessly sent to the younger sister in particular, can be seen in the surviving 1,500 letters.

'A female friend – amiable, clever and devoted – is a possession more valuable than parks or palaces'

Henrietta Temple by Disraeli

Above Selina, Countess of Bradford

Left Mary Anne Disraeli; painted in 1829 by F. Rochard

The great persuader

Above *Rival Stars*. Disraeli and Gladstone as represented in a *Punch* cartoon of 1868

Until he was 70, Disraeli held office only briefly: he was Chancellor of the Exchequer in three short-lived minority governments and Prime Minister for a few months in 1868. But he is remembered for his powerful speeches, passion and audacity. Disraeli was always assured of his genius and was persuasive in his ideas, yet his most sustained commitment was to his own political ambition.

Early political career

Disraeli first stood as a Radical Independent candidate for High Wycombe in 1832. Despite his confidence, he was defeated then and twice more by 1835. In 1835 he stood for Taunton and lost again.

In 1837 he was elected as Tory MP for Maidstone. His maiden speech was a disaster; he could hardly be heard above the derision and name-calling. Amid the cacophony he shouted, 'I shall sit down now but the time will come when you will hear me!'

His political commitment and sincerity were sometimes challenged; he was regarded as an impudent upstart and his sizeable debts became common knowledge. His Jewish heritage became a target for attack.

'My mind is a revolutionary mind. It is a continental mind. I am only great in action.'

Disraeli

Gladstone and Disraeli

William Gladstone was unimpressed on first meeting Disraeli, and his views never changed. Gladstone was serious, religious, hard-working and well-connected. He was respectable and accepted in a way that Disraeli could not be. Writing of the dinner party where they first met, Disraeli said that he found Gladstone 'rather dull, but we had a swan, very white and tender and stuffed with truffles, the best company there'.

Ambition and opportunity

Disraeli split the Tory party in the early 1840s, when he became the charismatic leader of 'Young England', a group of aristocratic dissidents fighting against the growing power of the middle class. He became increasingly critical of Peel; in 1846 the repeal of the Corn Laws gave him the opportunity to rail against Peel in Parliament for three hours. Disraeli voiced the anger and betrayal that many Conservatives felt, which contributed to Peel's resignation.

In 1847 Disraeli was elected MP for Buckingham and swiftly became leader of the Conservative party in the Commons in 1849, but served in opposition for most of the next twenty years.

The second Reform Bill in 1867 brought the vote to the working man. Much of the credit for passing the Act went to Disraeli and his position in the Conservative party was strengthened.

Above Participants in the Congress of Berlin, 1878

Prime Minister at last

Disraeli became Prime Minister for only nine months in 1868, then again from 1874 to 1880, two years after Mary Anne died. He was aged 70. During his second term he introduced progressive domestic policies such as the Public Health Act in 1875. In his political novels, most notably *Sybil, or the two Nations* (1840), he had outlined the need for reform.

The Empire

In foreign policy Disraeli was an imperialist keen to promote the presence and prestige of Britain. His personal romanticism and hard-fought quest for power influenced his vision, and he acted without full regard to his government. Disraeli's aggressive policies resulted in the acquisition of a major shareholding in the new Suez Canal in 1875. In 1876 he crowned Queen Victoria Empress of India, reinforcing Britain's position as an imperial power on the world stage.

Left Disraeli wearing his Garter insignia at the time of the Congress of Berlin in 1878

The Eastern Question

Disraeli's most celebrated triumph was at the Congress of Berlin in 1878. He had set out to prevent Russian expansion into Asia and to curtail its alliances with other nations. Through his skilful negotiations he achieved 'peace with honour' and was much fêted by politicians and the Queen as a result.

Rosette of Disraeli's colours
'I never made so many friends in my life or converted so many enemies. All the women are on my side and wear my colours, pink and white'.

The royal favourite

Disraeli had enormous respect for the monarchy and what it represented. He became a close and valued friend of Queen Victoria and her favourite Prime Minister. Throughout their considerable correspondence he was intimate but always respectful of her position and her views. He described the goings-on in Parliament to her as a colourful narrative; Gladstone, by contrast, addressed her 'as a public meeting'. When Queen Victoria was widowed, Disraeli consoled her and helped to bring her back into the public sphere.

Although the Queen was initially not impressed with Lord Derby's choice of Chancellor of the Exchequer in 1852, Disraeli made every effort to display his allegiance to her and to Prince Albert. He gradually won her respect and she acknowledged the hard won accomplishments of this perpetual outsider.

Flattery and wooing

Disraeli used every opportunity to flatter and woo the Queen. She enjoyed his display of romantic devotion and allowed herself to be cajoled and flattered; he was 'full of poetry, romance and chivalry'. Over time Disraeli developed a genuine fondness for the Queen that was fully reciprocated.

When he became Prime Minister, Disraeli always took time to guide the Queen through important questions raised in the Cabinet. Writing to her daily, he was often presenting information to his own advantage but the Queen appreciated his attentive care.

Empress of India

In 1876 Disraeli backed the Royal Titles Act, which enabled Queen Victoria to become Empress of India. It was a move calculated to halt Russian advances on India and make the Queen an equal to the Tsar. Queen Victoria had encouraged the Act, but Disraeli was criticised for prompting it without sufficient consultation.

Left *New Crowns for Old Ones.*
Disraeli offers the Queen the crown of India in a *Punch* cartoon of 1876

Above The Disraeli memorial in Hughenden church

Mourning his loss

After Disraeli died, Queen Victoria wrote: 'Never had I so kind and devoted a Minister, and very few such devoted friends.'

Protocol dictated that the Queen was unable to attend the funeral of one of her subjects, although the Prince of Wales was present. She sent a wreath of primroses bearing the words 'His favourite flowers, from Osborne, a tribute of affection from Queen Victoria'.

Queen Victoria made a pilgrimage to Hughenden on 30 April; she walked the route of his cortège, laid a wreath of china flowers on Disraeli's coffin and then spent time alone in his Study.

Her journal records: 'All was just the same as when, two and a half years ago, dear Lord Beaconsfield had received us there, such a sad contrast. We went into the library and drawing room where hangs my picture, all, all is the same only he is not there! ... I seemed to hear his voice and the impassioned, eager way he described everything.'

'You have heard me called a flatterer and it is true. Everyone likes flattery; and when you come to royalty, you should lay it on with a trowel.'

Disraeli

Above The royal visit to Hughenden in 1877

Right Bronze statuette of Queen Victoria at her spinning wheel by Sir Joseph Edgar Boehm, presented to Disraeli at his final audience on relinquishing office in 1880

Tour of the House

Disraeli believed that England was best ruled by traditional aristocratic families, living in grand country houses. He strived to be considered part of the landed gentry. Securing Hughenden Manor was vital to the realisation of his political ambitions and his personal aspirations.

Hughenden: the house

The location of Hughenden, and its proximity to Disraeli's father and sister at Bradenham Manor, made it desirable. He was attached to Buckinghamshire, enjoying the familiar landscapes and believed that in the 18th century: 'All the great statesmen of that period were born, or bred or lived in this great county.'

Buying the house

The house that the Disraelis acquired was a white, stuccoed three-storey building, dating from the 18th century. It belonged to the Norris family, with whom Disraeli was acquainted through living at Bradenham. It became available in 1846 at a price of £35,000, far exceeding Disraeli's budget. Lord George Bentinck and his brothers, Lord Titchfield and Lord Henry Bentinck, agreed to lend Disraeli £25,000 towards the cost, with the balance being borrowed from his bank and his solicitor.

Discussions regarding the sale were prolonged, with Disraeli finding obstacles to stall the proceedings, partly to raise further funds. Relations with the vendor's solicitors became strained, but finally in September 1848 Disraeli was able to write to his wife: 'It is all done and you are the Lady of Hughenden.'

He had been elected as member for Buckingham the previous year and now had all that he needed to become a leading political figure.

The transformation

Mary Anne took the lead in the transformation of Hughenden; in 1862 she consulted the architect Edward Buckton Lamb, whose work divided opinion. He was described as 'one of the most perverse and original of mid-Victorian British architects' and developed a large practice restoring and modernising country houses. Lamb removed the stucco to reveal the blue and red brickwork. He proposed a new parapet, with stepped battlements and pinnacles, and his own unusual design for window surrounds, made of red brick. Later, the architectural historian Nikolaus Pevsner commented: 'Lamb's details are excruciating, everything sharp, angular, aggressive ... the windowheads indescribable.'

A limited budget meant that change was compromised, and the essentially box-shaped 18th-century core of the house remained. For the Disraelis, however, it was a well-loved home. Lord Derby observed in 1865: 'D. Enjoys this place thoroughly and is never happier than when showing it to a friend.'

Parliament was in recess from the end of August until the New Year each year, enabling the Disraelis to spend their autumns at Hughenden. Disraeli's frequent ill health meant that it became an important retreat and place of recuperation. It also symbolised Disraeli's political credibility; it was his own country house estate.

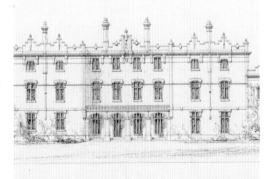

Left E.B. Lamb's proposed elevation for the north front, 1862

Left The garden at Hughenden in 1840; sepia drawing by John Norris (Bartolozzi Room).

Opposite The South Front from the fountain beds

The Entrance Arcade
The Entrance Hall

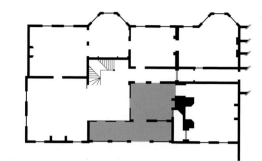

The Entrance Arcade

Here Mary Anne would greet her husband on his return from London. Disraeli inserted plate-glass windows and a tile pavement in order to create a more sheltered conservatory. In 1880 the arcade was filled with 'marble vases, busts, ferns and flowers'.

Decoration

The *ribbed ceiling*, which was painted to resemble oak, was added by Disraeli. The mahogany letterbox came from Disraeli's London home in Whitehall Gardens.

Sculpture

The *marble statue* of Disraeli is by Charles Bell Birch, ARA (1832–1903). It shows him as Chancellor of the Exchequer, wearing his Garter robes.

The *sculpture* opposite is *Edward Stanley, 14th Earl of Derby* by William Theed the Younger (1804–91). Derby was leader of the Conservatives in the Lords from 1846. Disraeli served as Chancellor in all three of his governments.

Right The Entrance Arcade

Opposite Disraeli, by Charles Bell Birch

Opposite far right Encaustic tiles on the cast-iron stove

The Entrance Hall

Look up, when entering the house: the ribbed plaster ceiling vaults form a striking feature. They were the first internal alterations that the Disraelis made and create a Gothic effect, popular in the mid-19th century.

The Entrance Hall is divided into two rooms separated by an arched opening. The brass and cast-iron stove, decorated with encaustic tiles, was installed for Disraeli, who hated the cold weather and was prone to chest complaints.

Decoration

The warm orange-red walls and grained woodwork follow the Disraelis' original design for this room.

Photographs

Disraeli's nephew and heir *Major Coningsby Disraeli*, MP, lived at Hughenden from 1892 until his death in 1936. There is also a photograph of Disraeli's brother Ralph, father of Coningsby (see p.44).

The Disraeli Room
The Garden Hall

The Disraeli Room

Mary Anne is thought to have used this as her morning room, on the sunny, south side of the house. After she died in 1872, the doorway into the Garden Hall was blocked up and it became the Housekeeper's Room. Coningsby Disraeli reopened the doorway and made it a morning room again.

Today the room provides an opportunity to learn more about Disraeli and a glimpse into the private life of a very public figure.

The Garden Hall

This room provided access to the garden terrace. Several of the portraits are of the personalities who influenced Disraeli as an adventurous and ambitious young man.

Paintings

The portrait of *Lord Byron* was painted by Richard Westall, RA, in 1813. Byron was a great influence on the young Disraeli, who travelled across Europe in his footsteps in 1829–31. Disraeli bought this portrait of his romantic hero. His father had inherited Byron's Venetian manservant Tita Falcieri, who had accompanied the poet's body back to Enland.

James Clay was a friend to the young, adventurous Disraeli. He was considered by Disraeli's family to be an unsuitable travelling companion, but they toured Europe together and embraced every experience. Clay was a notorious womaniser; he was little changed by marriage but kept his wife separate from his

Above **Portrait of Lord Byron by Richard Westall**

public life. He acknowledged all his children, however, and this portrait was given by his sons.

Edward Bulwer-Lytton, 1st Baron Lytton was influential in introducing Disraeli to high society. He was a novelist and somewhat of a dandy – 'the vainest man that perhaps ever existed', according to Disraeli.

The portrait of *Isaac D'Israeli*, was painted in 1777, when he was 11 years old.

Furniture

The 17th-century chair belonged to Isaac D'Israeli at Bradenham Manor. It is known as the *Abbot of Medmenham's chair*, although the abbey at Medmenham had been dissolved many years before it was made.

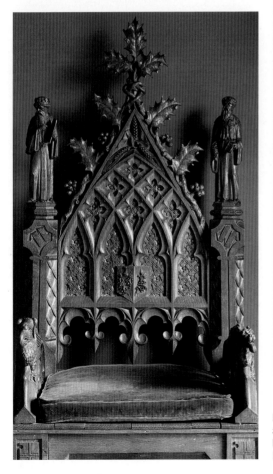

Mary Anne listed what she viewed as their different but complementary qualities:

Mary Anne on Disraeli	Mary Anne on Mary Anne
Very calm	Very effervescent
Manner grave and almost sad	Gay and happy-looking when speaking
Never irritable	Very irritable
Bad humoured	Good humoured
Warm in love but cold in friendship	Cold in love but warm in friendship
Very patient	No patience
Very studious	Very idle
Very generous	Only generous to those she loves
Often says what he does not think. It is impossible to find out who he likes or dislikes from his manner. He does not show his feelings.	Never says anything she does not think. Her manner is quite different, and to those she likes she shows her feelings.
No vanity	Much vanity
Conceited	No conceit
No self-love	Much self-love
He is seldom amused	Everything amuses her
He is a genius	She is a dunce
He is to be depended on to a certain degree	She is not to be depended on
His whole soul is devoted to politics and ambition	She has no ambition and hates politics

Left The neo-Gothic oak armchair was carved in 1863 by John Baldwin and bears Disraeli's coat of arms

The Drawing Room

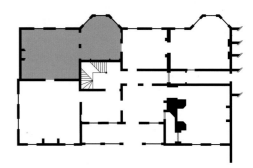

Disraeli used this room as his library. It was decorated with characteristically bold colours and ornamentation. On inheriting the house, his nephew Coningsby removed the oak bookcases to transform it into the present Drawing Room. More recent decoration has recaptured the busy richness of High Victorian style and the warm, domestic intimacy of the Disraelis.

Disraeli's marriage to Mary Anne began as one of convenience, but he became devoted to her and daily expressed feelings of gratitude, love and affection for her. As he later remarked: 'Health, my clear brain and your fond love – and I feel I can conquer the world.'

Decoration

The flock wallpaper was hung in 1948. It matches the colour, but not the pattern, of a previous paper. The woodwork has been regrained, but the plasterwork ceiling is thought to be original. The yellow silk curtains have been remade following the previous pattern, and the tassels and ties are original.

In old age, Disraeli would sit in this room, gazing into the fire and murmuring, 'Dreams! dreams! dreams!'

Pictures

Above the fireplace is an idealised portrait of *Mary Anne Disraeli* by J.G. Middleton, based on a miniature, also in this room. It was painted for Disraeli after his wife's death. He said of her: 'There was no care which she could not mitigate, and no difficulty which she could not face. She was the most cheerful and the most courageous woman I ever knew.'

The portrait on the left by the entrance door is *Alfred, Count D'Orsay* by John Wood. Count D'Orsay was an important friend to Disraeli at the start of his political career. He created a fashionable salon in Kensington with his wife's stepmother, the Countess of Blessington, and caused a scandal when he ran away to France with her. The Countess was a novelist and friend of Disraeli and Byron; her portrait also appears in this room.

Left The chiffonier

Below left An idealised portrait of Mary Anne: 'a perfect wife'

Below The chair was embroidered by Mary Anne with a 'B' for Beaconsfield

Furniture and ornaments

The marble *sculpture* is of Hero lighting the way for her lover Leander, by Ignazio Villa. It was presented to Disraeli by his great friend, the society hostess Lady Jersey, in 1865.

The French 18th-century gilt *chair* decorated with a coronet and the letter 'B' is one of a pair embroidered by Mary Anne to commemorate becoming Viscountess Beaconsfield in 1868. It demonstrates her obvious pride in being awarded the title.

The elaborate *chiffonier* (sideboard) is decorated with gilt bronze mounts and porcelain plaques of baskets of flowers. On the top is a pair of stoppered Meissen vases, decorated in high relief with fruit, flowers and butterflies. The chiffonier is very typical of Mary Anne's taste.

The Library
The Inner Entrance Hall

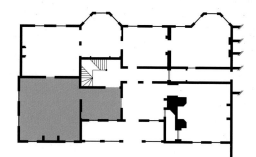

The Library

Disraeli inherited a love of books from his father, Isaac D'Israeli, a respected author and bibliophile. His father's collection amounted to over 25,000 well-catalogued volumes. When he died, Disraeli kept mainly works relating to theology, classics, history and some rare volumes on the Italian Renaissance. Many of the remaining books were sold to pay off some of Disraeli's mounting debts.

Decoration

Disraeli used this room as a drawing room, which Lord Ronald Gower described as 'a very gaudy apartment'. In the 1890s, Disraeli's nephew, Coningsby, turned the room into the current Library, lowering the ceiling and adding mahogany bookcases and doors. He also added the decorative plasterwork on the wall above the fireplace. The panels over the doors illustrate Aesop's fables of the fox and the crane.

Pictures

The portrait of Disraeli was painted free of charge by Sir Francis Grant and was given to Mary Anne in 1852, when Disraeli first became Chancellor of the Exchequer, aged 48.

Above The Library

Left The Carrara marble and scagliola (imitation marble) chimneypiece survives from the 18th-century room

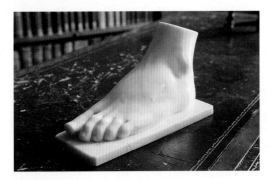

Sculpture

On the desk is a marble copy of Mary Anne's foot. Although this seems an unusual object today, copies of parts of the body were a popular form of Victorian ornament. Queen Victoria had several such objects at Osborne House, her country retreat on the Isle of Wight. The two plaster statuettes on top of the mantelpiece were given to Disraeli by Queen Victoria. They are after Sir Edwin Landseer, RA, and represent John Brown and Piper William Ross, her piper at Balmoral.

There are two 18th-century bronzed plaster busts over the doors of the Library: the figure of Alexander Pope at the entrance to the Hall, and John Milton over the door to the Drawing Room. Busts of famous literary figures were a common feature of country-house libraries.

Books

Disraeli had a passion both for reading books and writing them. When at Hughenden, he preferred to divide his time between working in his library and walking the estate. There are over 4000 volumes here, made up of Disraeli's own collection, selected works by his father and from his collection, and additions made by Coningsby.

The Library includes surprisingly few editions of Disraeli's own publications or proof copies of his novels. Some were sold after his death, but he was not a great collector of his own work. There are several foreign editions remaining, perhaps not as prized by book dealers. The collection reflects Disraeli's careers as politician (including 118 volumes of Hansard), and as novelist.

The Inner Entrance Hall

The portrait of *James D'Israeli*, Disraeli's brother, is by J.G. Middleton. James, known as Jem to the family, was sometimes petulant and demanding and an embarrassment to his brother. In response to one of his abrasive letters, Disraeli remarked, 'I don't mind the abuse, but I do the spelling'. He became a minor civil servant and, after his wife died, became involved with a Mrs Bassett and fathered at least one child by her.

Hanging nearby is a portrait of *Edward Stanley*, 14th Earl of Derby. He was Prime Minister three times and Disraeli served as Chancellor of the Exchequer in each of his administrations.

The portrait of *Lord Lyndhurst* is by Alfred, Count D'Orsay and Sir Edwin Landseer. Lyndhurst was Tory Lord Chancellor and one of Disraeli's first influential friends. This portrait first belonged to Gladstone.

Sculpture

The two marble busts show Disraeli in his youth. His face is framed by soft ringlets and he appears a romantic figure.

Above The ornately bound copy of Goethe's *Faust* was a Christmas gift to Disraeli from Queen Victoria in 1876

Above left Marble copy of Mary Anne's foot

Above right The Queen's manservant John Brown

The Dining Room

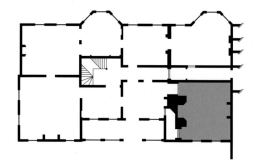

The Disraelis entertained frequently but modestly. Menus were written in French, and food was brought to each diner in sequential courses (*service à la russe*). This innovation to dining was introduced to England in the 19th century and was less ostentatious than presenting all the delicacies simultaneously.

Decoration

The neo-Gothic ceiling of wooden ribs and papier-mâché Tudor rosettes was probably put up early in the 19th century by the previous owner, John Norris. The fitted oak sideboard and wooden arch decorated with shields and spandrels were probably installed at the same time.

Dinner is served

Generally the meals were not ambitious but rather plain – surprisingly, given the Disraelis' fondness for flamboyant display. Turtle soup, turbot, lamb chops and chicken supreme with asparagus were typical dishes served.

Friends often sent special foods as gifts, such as lobster from Mrs Brydges Willyams in Devon and 'a battalion of pheasants' from Anthony de Rothschild at Aston Clinton.

At their London house in Grosvenor Gate the Disraelis hosted dinner parties of up to 60 MPs; guests at Hughenden were fewer but significant, including Queen Victoria, who came to lunch in 1877. As the Queen was of short stature, the legs of one of the dining chairs were specially cut down to enable her to reach the floor comfortably.

When dining alone, the Disraelis ate relatively little, often missing breakfast but having a buffet lunch at noon. Disraeli had a small appetite by Victorian standards and in later life Mary Anne developed stomach cancer and suffered prolonged periods of illness.

Left Menu for a banquet at Grosvenor Gate

Right The Dining Room, showing the portrait of Queen Victoria by George Koberwein, after Heinrich von Angeli

Paintings

This room contains paintings of some of the people closest to Disraeli, including portraits of his father and grandfather. To the left of the fireplace is a portrait of Montagu Corry, Baron Rowton. It was painted by Heinrich von Angeli in 1877. Corry was Disraeli's Principal Private Secretary from 1866 and his most loyal and trusted aide. According to a contemporary, 'He gave the Prime Minister all the gossip of the clubs and all the chatter of the drawing rooms'. After Disraeli died, his papers were left in Corry's safe hands.

Queen Victoria commissioned a replica of a portrait of herself to present to Disraeli in 1876. The original hangs in Buckingham Palace. He was anxious to have an image of the woman he called 'The Faery' in his 'Gallery of Affection'.

The original of the portrait of Disraeli was painted for Queen Victoria at her request and is at Windsor. Lord Gower described the portrait as 'terribly and painfully like'. This replica was painted for the Queen to present to Disraeli.

To the right of the fireplace is a portrait of Sir Philip Rose by Piet van Havermeet. Rose was Disraeli's lifelong friend, political agent, executor and trustee, who brought order into his finances.

Sculpture

Over the sideboard, there are five white, 17th-century, marble reliefs by Orazio Marinali. They probably once formed part of a frieze on the principal staircase at Palazzo Grimani in Venice, demolished in 1820. Sir Philip Rose gave Disraeli ten of the original set of sixteen, but they were sold from Hughenden in 1881. With generous help from the Art Fund, the National Trust was able to buy back the five shown here, in 1994.

Left The Earl of Beaconsfield in 1877; a copy by Robert Muller of the portrait painted by Heinrich von Angeli for Queen Victoria

Above 17th-century marble reliefs over the sideboard representing the passions by Orazio Marinali

The Staircase
The South Bedroom
The Boudoir

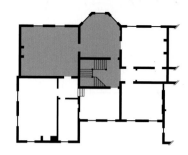

The Staircase

After Mary Anne died in 1872, Hughenden became a quieter, sadder place. In the Entrance Hall and up the staircase Disraeli surrounded himself with portraits of literary friends, beautiful women and political allies. He called it his 'Gallery of Affection'.

Although much smaller in scale, the 'Gallery of Affection' at Hughenden echoes Sir Robert Peel's 'Gallery of Famous Men', established at Drayton Manor in Staffordshire in the 1830s, which was a forerunner to the National Portrait Gallery, founded in 1856.

The South Bedroom

This was the Disraelis' bedroom and has been re-created with the help of the 1881 inventory. The inventory indicates that more rooms existed; it is likely that the Disraelis each had their own suite of rooms. The west wing (now housing offices and accommodation) incorporated further bedrooms, dressing rooms, water closets and a bridal room. Servant accommodation was provided in the second floor.

Below left The Staircase

Below right The South Bedroom

The Boudoir

This room and the South Bedroom have been re-created with the help of the 1881 inventory, which provides a snapshot of Hughenden at the time of Disraeli's death. In 1893 the Boudoir was described as a 'bright little bow windowed place of light blue not unrelieved by red'. The room is seen as a work place for Mary Anne, equivalent to Disraeli's study. She may well have managed her household accounts here and devised plans for the transformation of the garden.

Left 'Osborne 1865 or Sorrow'. Prince Albert's death in 1861 provoked Queen Victoria's long and intense widowhood; engraving after Sir Edwin Landseer

Decoration

The room was refurbished in 1995. The yellow silk curtains are as described in the inventory. The wallpaper was made by Cole & Son from original Victorian printing blocks in their collection.

The carpet is a velvet worsted wool Wilton and is based on a fragment from a 19th-century Wilton carpet found at Balcarres in Fife. The refurbishment was made possible with the support of local National Trust Centres and Associations and generous individual donations.

Furniture

The furniture is mostly original. The bed is modern, but is similar to the white iron bedstead described in the inventory. The chairs are covered in the same yellow silk as the bed hangings.

Pictures

There are several portraits of Queen Victoria and her family in this room. Over the fireplace are lithographs of Queen Victoria and Prince Albert in joined twin oval gilt frames. They were signed and presented by Queen Victoria. The Queen appears on horseback in two pictures; as a young girl and later with John Brown after the death of her husband.

Pictures

Many of the pictures in this room can be found listed in the 1881 inventory. Amongst others, there are portraits of Queen Victoria's daughters, Princess Alice, Princess Victoria and Princess Beatrice; further portraits of the Queen, Prince Albert and their children appear in the South Bedroom.

The pen drawing of the monument to Isaac D'Israeli is by its architect, Edward Buckton Lamb. This memorial to Disraeli's father is visible from the window in this room. His portrait appears next to the drawing and is by Daniel Maclise.

Furniture

The kneehole desk or dressing table is mahogany and dates from the early 18th century. In the mid-19th century such items were often used with a free-standing mirror on top. The secretaire pullout is also mahogany and has typically late 18th-century handles.

The vellum-topped table is pine. It was possibly adapted to show the top. Underneath is written, 'This table finished 1813.'

The Study

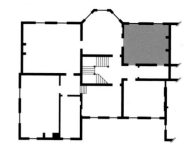

In a letter to Lady Bradford, Disraeli referred to this room as 'My Workshop'. In later life he would work at the desk in the mornings on his political papers and correspondence with his secretary, Monty Corry. From here he also wrote lively letters to his female friends and worked on his later novels, *Lothair*, *Endymion* and *Falconet*. When Queen Victoria visited Hughenden after Disraeli's death, she asked to spend some time alone in this room.

Decoration

The room is the least changed in the house since Disraeli's time. By studying the 1881 photograph, it was possible to reproduce the patterns of carpets and wallpaper. The fireplace tiles were the inspiration for the colours chosen for the Brussels weave carpet, rewoven in 1983.

Disraeli favoured this room to work in, as it was easy to keep warm, and he hated to work in the cold: 'This paper in the country is always damp, the ink thick, and pens consequently incompetent.'

Above The Study today

Left The Study in 1881

Pictures

Portraits of both Disraeli's parents appear in this room, painted by John Downman. They are watercolours, completed the year after Disraeli was born. Over the fireplace is a portrait of his mother, Maria, and his father Isaac's portrait hangs over the writing desk.

A print of a pen drawing of Isaac D'Israeli can also be seen, entitled 'Author of Life and Character of Charles I'.

On the wall opposite the fireplace is a set of seven watercolour views of Potsdam in Germany. They were presented to Disraeli by the Princess Royal, the eldest daughter of Queen Victoria and wife of the future Emperor of Germany.

Furniture

The furniture is original to the room. Behind the desk, the bobbin-turned chair was specially made for Disraeli in High Wycombe, historically the centre of the British chair-making industry. The trolley is known as 'gypsy ware'. On it stands the red dispatch box that Disraeli used when Chancellor of the Exchequer.

On the desk is the writing slope that Disraeli had used since his school days. There is also a gilt bronze inkstand that was a gift from his lifelong friend Lady Londonderry. The black-edged notepaper on the desk was always used by Disraeli after Mary Anne's death in 1872.

Below Disraeli's writing desk in his Study

The Statesman's Room
The Bartolozzi Room

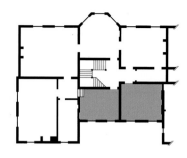

The Statesman's Room

This was originally a bedroom, but now has items relating to the Congress of Berlin, held in June–July 1878. It was convened by the major European nations to restore the balance of power in the Balkans following the Russo-Turkish war of 1877–8. The congress awarded Cyprus to Britain and was Disraeli's greatest triumph in foreign policy and possibly in his political career.

Queen Victoria advised Disraeli not to attend the conference as he was 73 and in frail health. However, once in Berlin, his skilful oratory so impressed the delegates that the chair of the congress, Prince Otto von Bismarck, was moved to declare 'Der alte Jude, das is der Mann' ('The old Jew, he is the man').

Furniture

Disraeli's satinwood reading desk is inlaid with red velvet. It is similar in style to reading desks in synagogues, and he would stand at it to read. The desk came originally from 19 Curzon Street, Disraeli's London home at the end of his life.

Below A cherrywood fan, signed by the participants at the Congress of Berlin

The Bartolozzi Room

This is the name given in the 1881 inventory. It possibly refers to the wallpaper, which had a printed pattern similar to the work of the 18th-century engraver Francesco Bartolozzi.

Textiles

The black silk robe of the Chancellor of the Exchequer is believed to have been made for William Pitt the Younger in the 18th century. When Disraeli first put it on in 1852, a judge remarked that he would find it uncommonly heavy, but he replied: 'Oh, I find it uncommonly light'. Notoriously, Disraeli refused to give up the robe to Gladstone, his successor. So after prolonged and heated correspondence, Gladstone was forced to have another made.

The scarlet and ermine robe lined with white silk taffeta was worn by Disraeli when he was raised to the peerage as Earl of Beaconsfield in 1876. Next to the robes are his leather court shoes with gold buckles and his court sword.

Pictures

These include pen-and-ink drawings by E.B. Lamb of his designs for Hughenden.

Above One of three sepia drawings of Hughenden Manor in 1840 by John Norris, the previous owner, showing the house before it was remodelled

Left Detail of the black silk robe with gold braid worn by Disraeli as Chancellor of the Exchequer

Below stairs

Mary Anne Disraeli took responsibility for most of the day-to-day running of the households at Hughenden and Grosvenor Gate in London. She hated waste and extravagance and was meticulous in her efforts to reduce her husband's debts.

Keeping account of the servants

Mary Anne noted all her expenditure in eleven large account books, now held at the Bodleian Library in Oxford. She also recorded the names and wages of her servants and detailed reasons for hiring and firing them. Hughenden was a relatively modest household, employing no more than six or seven servants plus a coachman and two gardeners at any one time.

There were regular servants' balls. In 1855 Disraeli wrote to Mrs Brydges Willyams in Devon: 'Our household and their guests were dancing till past five o'clock this morning; you must have heard the fiddle, I think, at Torquay.'

Entertaining guests

Although Hughenden was a small house compared to those of Disraeli's political colleagues, he entertained frequently. During September 1862 he listed the following guests: 'Lord and Lady Salisbury, Sir William and Lady Georgina Codrington, Lord and Lady Godolphin Osbourne, Lord and Lady Curzon, Lord Stanley, Lord St Asaph, Colonel and Mrs Fane, Baron Rothschild of Paris and many others. It's as hard work as having a playhouse or keeping an inn.'

The rooms below stairs

We can gain some understanding of life below stairs at Hughenden from 19th-century inventories. There are also other sources. A book found in the Library entitled *The Companion to the Orchard* by Henry Phillips (London, 1831) is inscribed 'Servants Library Hughenden Manor', suggesting that this might be a sole survivor of a lost servants' library.

There were rooms for the butler and housekeeper, pantries and a boot room below stairs, and evidence that Disraeli kept a well-stocked wine cellar. The 150-feet-deep well supplied water for drinking, washing, cooking and flushing water closets. Water was drawn using buckets and a winch.

The boiler room contained an iron boiler stoked with wood and coal. Pipes and stoves were installed to supply hot water and heat throughout the house, as Disraeli hated feeling cold.

In Disraeli's time, the kitchen was on the ground floor next to the Dining Room and contained a seven-foot open kitchen range. It was relocated in the 1900s by Coningsby to the newly constructed west wing, which contained new servants' quarters.

Extracts from Mary Anne's accounts

May 1858

1st   Received from Mrs Rowles 5£ which she had on account.
Mrs Rowles leaves my service for no fault only she is too young to be competent for housekeeping. Very sweet temper and dresses hair beautifully, perfectly honest.

6th One Marsella bin 6

February 1859

4th Henry Green discharged for being often intoxicated.
Anne Chard left my service this day nearly 3 years with us, goes with no fault but to keep her Uncle's house.

The Strong Room door

The Garden

Hughenden offered a restful retreat from the pressures of London for the Disraelis. Redesigning and replanting the garden and wider estate were vital to their vision of a country house estate. Hughenden became an engaging project for them both.

Under Mary Anne Disraeli's enthusiastic instruction, the garden was redesigned at the same time as the house, in 1862. At the age of 73 Mary Anne worked outside all day, supervising progress: 'Hughenden is now a chaos, for Mary Anne is now making a new garden. She never loved the old one, and now she has more than twenty navvies at work, levelling and making terraces.'

Her design shows an Italian influence, incorporating a pergola stretching the length of the house, enriched with classical statuary and urns from Florence and Venice. Mary Anne's close involvement may have been partly a consequence of financial constraints, but also echoes a growing contemporary interest in amateur garden planning and design. The result was a garden and estate reflecting the interests and passions of its owners, rather than the style of a famous designer.

When the National Trust took on the care of Hughenden Manor in 1947, the gardens were little more than hay meadows. Using photographs from 1881 they have been restored to a popular 19th-century 'Gardenesque' style, reflecting the taste and vision of its former owners.

Right The house from the fountain beds

1 The South Terrace and Lawn

Disraeli enjoyed walking along the terrace and feeding his peacocks, as befitted a gentleman at home on his country estate. After his death, the peacocks were bequeathed to Queen Victoria and a number of his friends.

Mary Anne's iron pergola was lost to salvage during the Second World War. Climbing shrubs such as jasmine and wisteria now grow against the warm south wall, whilst the beds closest to the house retain an Italianate structure and style, supplemented with bedding plants. They include Mediterranean shrubs such as cypress, which featured in Mary Anne's original design.

The lawn is punctuated with colourful island beds and a fountain at the far end. The bedding scheme is changed in spring and summer each year, using 8,000 plants per season.

2 The Fountain

Excavation has revealed that the fountain was never intended as a water feature, probably due to its windy and exposed location. Instead, its bowls are filled with displays of annuals, drawing your eye the length of the garden from the house.

In Mary Anne's time, the six beds encircling the fountain were planted mainly with 'Microfolia' roses sent by Mrs Brydges Willyams from Devon. Today, a vibrant bedding scheme reflects Mary Anne's taste for strong colour contrast.

Surrounding the lawn is a high-growing box hedge in semi-natural shapes with added specimen trees. This evergreen backdrop encloses the garden, protecting it from wind and frost, as well as showing the statues to advantage.

Numbers refer to the map of the estate on the inside front cover.

Above The garden in 1881

Left Statue on the South Terrace

The North Lawn
The Pleasure Gardens

3 The North Lawn

In contrast to the Victorian bedding schemes of the South Lawn, the entrance to the property exhibits the Victorian fascination for collecting exotic trees. The specimen conifers on the North Lawn include Chilean Yew and Cypress Cedar. Mary Anne believed that each conifer should grow with sufficient space to display its individual beauty. They are surrounded by an oval carriage drive with a backdrop of evergreen shrubs. The trees make a dramatic entrance to the property, but need to be replaced every 40 years to ensure that they do not obscure the house completely.

'A forest is like the Ocean, monotonous only to the ignorant. It is a life of ceaseless variety.'

Disraeli

4 The Pleasure Grounds

The formal garden gives way to the Pleasure Grounds at the southern end. This area provided a managed, natural space for Disraeli. It combines a soft canopy of trees with the additional interest of island beds and more formal planting. The Pleasure Grounds offer a shaded walk amidst evergreen shrubs and naturalised bulbs in the spring. A view of the wider valley can be glimpsed between trees.

Above The Pleasure Grounds

Left The conifer collection

The Arboretum
The German Forest

5 The Arboretum

Disraeli loved to plant trees to commemorate a friend's visit or an occasion. To the east of the garden the Arboretum is planted with around 80 specimen shrubs and trees. As much as 40% of the planting was lost during the storms of 1987 and 1990; many had been planted in Disraeli's time. The planting is a mixture of evergreen and deciduous trees and includes sweet chestnuts and cedars, known to be amongst Disraeli's favourites.

6 The German Forest

The German Forest is an expression of Disraeli's passion for trees. Planted with conifers such as larch, Douglas fir and cedars, it was designed to resemble the vast forests of northern Bohemia. At Hughenden, the planting also includes yew and laurel so that the overall effect and the way that it is managed are more in the style of mixed woodland. The notion of a German Forest, however, expresses Disraeli's sense of romance and grandeur. He enjoyed exploring the curving pathways through his trees and liked to monitor their growth and health, often taking with him a hatchet to remove unwanted ivy.

Disraeli was also fascinated by the lives and work of woodsmen: 'Their conversation is most interesting.... I don't know any men who are so complete masters of their business, and of the secluded, but delicious world in which they live.'

'I have a passion for books and trees; I like to look at them. When I come down [to the country] I spend the first week in sauntering about my park, examining all the trees...'

Disraeli

Top Disraeli enjoying his woodland

Above Woodsmen at Hughenden, 1870

The Walled Garden
The Stableyard

7 The Walled Garden

This garden was originally established in 1754 to supply fruit and vegetables to the house. The practice continued well into the 20th century, but by the 1950s the garden had become derelict. Its walls were repaired in the 1960s, and a new glasshouse was added a decade later. In the 1980s the current range of apple trees was planted, a wide variety of old English types. More recently, a restored Victorian vine house, complete with five descendents of the Black Hamburg vine at Hampton Court, has been added.

There are no surviving photographs, plans or drawings of the main walled garden, but archaeological research has identified key pathways and borders. The current layout reflects what is known about the original design. No details have survived concerning the actual use of the garden, rendering a complete reconstruction impossible.

However, this has provided new opportunities for learning. The Walled Garden has been developed as a space for experimentation and discovery, for visitors, horticultural students and National Trust staff and volunteers alike. Old and new methods are tried for growing traditional crops and visitors, along with staff and volunteers, discover the joys of 'growing your own'.

Opposite right The coach door

Opposite far right A selection of produce grown is supplied to the restaurant

Left Experimenting with growing spaces in the Walled Garden

8 The Stableyard

The stableyard buildings were created by E.B. Lamb in 1866–8. Sadly, it was the last commissioned work that he completed before being declared bankrupt while building a country home for his retirement. He died in 1869.

The stableyard housed Mary Anne's pony and cart for her trips into High Wycombe. The pony was a gift from Sir Philip Rose. Both she and Disraeli also used the pony cart to drive around the park when they became too frail to walk.

Currently the visitor reception, restaurant and shop are located here. On display at Hughenden is a Victorian coach door, painted with the Beaconsfield and Viney arms. It commemorates a poignant story. When the Disraelis were climbing into the coach on their way to Westminster, Mary Anne's thumb became trapped in the door. Despite the pain, she said nothing, so as not to disturb her husband's preparation for an important speech. After he had alighted, she fainted. When Disraeli heard later what had happened, he preserved the coach door as a reminder of his wife's devotion and stoicism.

During the Second World War, when the house was requisitioned by the War Office, several motorised vehicles were housed here.

The Estate

The Disraelis purchased Hughenden as much for the landscape as for the house. Disraeli had come under increasing pressure to own a country estate in order to improve his standing as a serious politician. Once established at Hughenden, he immersed himself in the role of country squire, but he had no taste for the associated pursuits of hunting and shooting.

The estate is a combination of ancient forest and open valley parkland. The parkland is less than 200 years old and was planted by John Norris in the 1820s with limes, horse chestnuts, walnuts and sycamores. When Disraeli acquired it, the estate extended to 750 acres, but he soon enlarged it to 1,400 acres, increasing his debts still further.

A country retreat

The Disraelis' life at Hughenden can be seen in contrast to their very public, noisy existence in London. Disraeli valued the solitude that Hughenden offered and the opportunity to become absorbed in the restorative beauty of the natural world. Unlike Gladstone, who had a reputation for felling trees, Disraeli liked to plant and walk amongst them.

As part of the improvements to the estate, Disraeli created an ornamental pond in 1862, adding two swans, romantically named Hero and Leander. He also introduced a new carriage drive in 1870, providing a simple and unpretentious approach to the house. Funding the changes required additional revenue, and estate tenants saw their rents increase considerably.

9 The Monument

The 50-foot-high memorial to Disraeli's father, Isaac, was commissioned by Mary Anne as a surprise gift in 1852. The obelisk was constructed from Bath stone by E.B. Lamb at a cost of £500 and is clearly visible from the house. It was restored by the National Trust with grant-aid from English Heritage and Wycombe District Council.

10 Hughenden church

The earliest parts of the existing church are the chancel and north chapel, which are 13th- or 14th-century, but a church has stood on the site since the 12th century. During 1874–5, Disraeli decided that it should be almost entirely rebuilt.

On the north side there is a memorial to Disraeli from Queen Victoria in 1881. It contains a line from Proverbs reading: 'Kings love him that speaketh right'.

Disraeli wanted to be buried at Hughenden, by the east end of the north chapel, rather than in Westminster Abbey; this request was supported by Victoria, who claimed that his 'wishes to be laid by the side of his devoted wife should be considered as sacred, and that he should rest at Hughenden, which he was so fond of'.

The modern estate

Since 1986 the National Trust has been slowly acquiring land that once belonged to the Hughenden estate. It is a tenant-farmed landscape combining arable and pasture regimes. Conservation grazing is promoted by the National Trust on the estate as an effective way of encouraging biodiversity.

The estate continues to provide a green retreat for the inhabitants of nearby High Wycombe. It is also home to many protected and unusual species.

Above The D'Israeli Monument

Left Disraeli's funeral

Far left The protected Striped Lychnis moth (*Shargacucullia lychnitis*) is found in limited numbers here.

After Disraeli

After Disraeli's death in 1881, Hughenden Manor reverted to the quiet obscurity that it had previously enjoyed.

Coningsby Disraeli

At Disraeli's funeral there were only two surviving members of his immediate family: his brother Ralph and Ralph's son, Coningsby, heir to Hughenden Manor. Coningsby was only fourteen in 1881, so it was decided to rent out the house until he came into his inheritance. Any items that Disraeli had not specifically marked as heirlooms were sold.

Sir Samuel Wilson, a civil engineer and a loyal Conservative, became the new tenant at Hughenden. He was able to buy several items from the house at the Christie's sale, and the decoration of Hughenden remained much the same whilst Wilson lived there. When Coningsby inherited Hughenden at the age of 26, he bought many of the items from Wilson and over the next 44 years made radical changes to the house.

In 1904 Coningsby moved the kitchen into a new service wing to the south-west corner of the house. He also installed modern plumbing and electricity. Disraeli's Drawing Room became the Library; Coningsby installed new bookcases and lowered the ceiling to a mezzanine floor, which meant losing the State Bedroom above it.

Coningsby became a major in the Royal Buckinghamshire Hussars. He was also an Alderman and Justice of the Peace. He served as the Conservative MP for Altrincham from 1892 until 1906, but did not have an outstanding political career.

After Coningsby

When Coningsby Disraeli died in 1936, he had no heir to inherit Hughenden, and his widow Marion moved out of the house. Disraeli's niece Mrs Calverley sold Hughenden to W.H. Abbey, who entrusted the house and 189 acres of land to the Disraelian Society to be preserved for the nation.

Like many country houses, Hughenden Manor was requisitioned and occupied by the military during the Second World War and made a vital contribution to the war effort.

Above Her Majesty Queen Elizabeth in the Dining Room during her private visit to Hughenden in April 1938

Left The carved wooden chimneypiece in the Dining Room, decorated with Disraeli's motto, *Forti Nihil Difficile*, was inserted by Coningsby Disraeli.

Opposite Major Coningsby Disraeli, heir to Hughenden Manor

Top Secret Hughenden

During the Second World War Hughenden housed a vital and top secret mapping unit, codenamed 'Hillside'. Its purpose was to create accurate target maps for RAF bombing missions over Germany and occupied Europe. By 1941 it had become clear that with the rough maps then available, only a small proportion of bombs were falling within even five miles of their target. Thousands of bomber crews' lives were being lost to no purpose. More accurate maps were needed.

Making the maps

Situated near Bomber Command headquarters, Hughenden Manor was requisitioned by the Air Ministry in 1941. As the RAF didn't have specialist mapmakers, a team of Royal Engineers were called in, using old German road maps as a starting point. From these they drew and painted new maps, adding up-to-date landmarks found from aerial reconnaissance photos, viewed in 3D through a stereoscope. Woods were coloured a dark green, fields were grey and rivers a silvery colour, as they would appear in moonlight on a night bombing raid. Roads were coloured red using ox blood as paint. This was found to show up best when the maps were photographed for printing the bomber crews' copies, but the paint pots had to be kept covered to prevent the flies eating the paint.

Above Drawing Office no. 1

Left Bombing raid map of Munster

Maps were made not only for targets in cities like Berlin, Hamburg and Dresden, but also for strategic missions including the Dam Busters raid, the V1 and V2 rocket factory at Peenemunde, the battleship *Tirpitz* and the Eagle's Nest, Hitler's mountain retreat.

Life at Hillside

Civilian artists, architects and draughtsmen, male and female, were recruited from all over the country into the RAF to boost numbers as operations expanded. As at Bletchley Park, the code-breaking centre, many of these retained their unconventional and somewhat bohemian approach to life, even when in uniform.

Above The *Hillside Herald* was an in-house newsletter, produced to keep up morale. It was stopped after the 12th edition because of the risk to security

Left Distribution and dispatch

The National Trust

In 1947 the Abbey family and the Disraelian Society gave Hughenden Manor to the National Trust. The house was soon redecorated and adapted to become a Disraeli museum, but there was little change for 30 years. During this time, the house and garden began to look rather tired and neglected.

Restoration

In 1983 it was decided to restore Hughenden. It was not possible to represent Hughenden exactly as it had been in Disraeli's time. Many of the items relating to the lives of the Disraelis had been dispersed, and the building changes made by Coningsby Disraeli precluded setting back the clock completely.

The restoration, led by the late Christopher Wall, was informed by detailed research into old photographs and the property inventories. Archived letters from visitors to Hughenden that described specific rooms were a valuable resource, and the National Trust also made use of up-to-date research into the subtleties of mid-Victorian style and design.

To supplement actual research findings, sympathetic colours, fabrics, paint finishes and carpets were selected. The intention was to create an atmosphere in which the Disraelis could consider themselves at home.

Right Conservation
cleaning in action

Bibliography

The Hughenden Papers are on deposit in the Bodleian Library, Oxford. The late Christopher Wall's June 1993 report on the redecoration of the house between 1983 and 1990 and Bronwen Thomas's 1994 landscape survey of the estate are in the Trust files at Hughenden.

ANON., 'English Homes, No.xxii', *Illustrated London News*, 22 April 1893.

ANON., 'Hughenden Manor revived', *Apollo*, April 2002, p.8.

BATTERSEA, Constance, *Reminiscences*, London, 1922.

BLAKE, Robert, *Disraeli*, London, 1966.

BOGDANOR, Vernon, 'Benjamin Disraeli', *Writers and their Houses*, London, 1993, pp. 172–80.

BRADFORD, Sarah, *Disraeli*, London, 1982.

CORNFORTH, John, 'Hughenden Manor, Buckinghamshire,' *Country Life*, 11 February 1993, pp.40–3.

GOWER, Lord Ronald, *My Reminiscences*, London, 1895, 2 vols [the original MS of Gower's account of his visits to Hughenden was sold at Sotheby's, 12–13 December 1977, lot 324].

HARDWICK, Molly, *Mrs Dizzy: The Life of Mary Anne Disraeli, Viscountess Beaconsfield*, London, 1972.

HIBBERT, Christopher, *Disraeli and his World*, London, 1978.

HOLLOWAY, John, *The Victorian Sage*, London, 1953. pp.86–110.

KELSALL, Malcolm, *The Great Good Place: The Country House and English Literature*, Hemel Hempstead, 1993, pp. 124–37.

KESSLER, David, 'The Rothschilds and Disraeli in Buckinghamshire', *Transactions of the Jewish History Society of England*, xxix, 1982–6, pp.231–52.

MCARDELL, Frederick, 'The Account Books of "a Perfect Wife"', *Country Life*, 24 December 1981, pp.2252–3.

MILES, Paul, 'Peacocks and Primroses: Disraeli's Garden at Hughenden Manor, Buckinghamshire,' *Country Life*, 28 January 1982, pp.216–7.

MONYPENNY, W. F., and BUCKLE, G.E., *The Life of Benjamin Disraeli, Earl of Beaconsfield*, London, 1910–20, 6 vols.

SWARTZ, Helen M. and Marvin, ed., *Disraeli's Reminiscences*, New York, 1975.

SYKES, James, *Mary Anne Disraeli: The Story of Viscountess Beaconsfield*, London, 1928.

WEINTRAUB, Stanley, *Disraeli: A Biography*, London, 1993.

WIEBE, M. G., ed., *Benjamin Disraeli Letters*, Toronto, 1982–.

ZETLAND, The Marquis of, ed., *The Letters of Disraeli to Lady Bradford and Lady Chesterfield*, London, 1929, 2 vols.

Acknowledgements

This new guidebook has been written by Sally Stafford, to whom the National Trust is very grateful. I would also like to thank curator for Hughenden, Charles Pugh, and all the staff and volunteers at Hughenden who have contributed in various ways, in particular Martin Stephen.

Oliver Garnett

Illustrations

Mary Evans Picture Library pp.14–15, 15 (top right), 39 (top); National Trust pp.3 (top), 8 (centre and bottom right), 12 (top right), 13 (bottom right), 30 (bottom left), 37 (top right); NT/David Watson pp.8 (bottom left), 16, 23 (centre right), 34–5, 36, 38 (top and bottom), 39 (bottom), 40, 41 (left and right), 42 (bottom left), 43 (top right), 45 (top), 46 (left and right), 47 (top and bottom), 48; National Trust Photo Library pp.2, 7 (bottom left); NTPL/Matthew Antrobus p.18; NTPL/John Bethell p.23 (bottom left); NTPL/Vera Collingwood p.37 (bottom left); NTPL/Andreas von Einsiedel pp.8 (top right), 14 (bottom left), 19 (bottom left), 22, 23 (top and bottom right), 24 (top and bottom), 25 (top left and centre), 26–7, 27 (top right), 28 (bottom left and centre), 30 (top right), 31, 33 (left), back cover; NTPL/John Hammond front cover, pp.1, 3 (bottom right), 4–5, 7 (top right), 11 (bottom right), 12 (bottom right), 13 (top), 15 (bottom right), 17 (top and bottom), 19 (right), 21, 27 (bottom left), 29, 32, 33 (top right), 44, 45 (bottom); NTPL/Angelo Hornak p.9; NTPL/Nick Pollard pp.6, 10, 11 (top left), 20, 43 (bottom left); Photo Library pp.42–3.

High-quality prints from the extensive and unique collections of the National Trust Photo Library are available at **www.ntprints.com**

The National Trust

is a registered charity

is independent of government

was founded in 1895 to preserve places of historic interest or natural beauty permanently for the benefit of the nation

relies on the generosity of its supporters, through membership subscriptions, gifts, legacies and the contribution of many tens of thousands of volunteers

protects and opens to the public over 300 historic houses and gardens and 49 industrial monuments and mills

owns more than 255,000 hectares (630,000 acres) of the most beautiful countryside and over 710 miles of outstanding coast for people to enjoy

If you would like to become a member or make a donation, please telephone 0844 800 1895 (minicom 0844 800 4410); write to The National Trust, PO Box 39, Warrington WA5 7WD; alternatively, see our website at **www.nationaltrust.org.uk**

© 2010 The National Trust

Revised 2012

Registered charity number 205846

ISBN 978-1-84359-319-5

Text by Sally Stafford

Designed by McGillan Eves

Bird's-eye view by Andrew Macdonald

Printed by Park Lane Press for National Trust (Enterprises) Ltd, Heelis, Kemble Drive, Swindon, Wilts SN2 2NA on Cocoon Silk made from 100% recycled paper

The home of the most unlikely Victorian Prime Minister

Meet the dandy who became a statesman.

Explore the newly flourishing Walled Garden.

Discover the enduring love story of Disraeli and Mary Anne.

Share Hughenden's 'Top Secret' past.

ISBN 978-1-843

KR-879-551

9 781843 5